Many Small
Hungerings

Also by William Bortz

The Grief We're Given
The Sky Grew Back with Clouds

Many Small Hungerings

Poetry

WILLIAM BORTZ

Andrews McMeel
PUBLISHING®

Andrews McMeel Publishing
a division of Andrews McMeel Universal
1130 Walnut Street, Kansas City, Missouri 64106

www.andrewsmcmeel.com

23 24 25 26 27 VEP 10 9 8 7 6 5 4 3 2 1

ISBN: 978-1-5248-7979-2

Library of Congress Control Number: 2022949706

Editor: Patty Rice
Art Director: Julie Barnes
Designer: Tiffany Meairs
Production Editor: Dave Shaw
Production Manager: Julie Skalla

ATTENTION: SCHOOLS AND BUSINESSES
Andrews McMeel books are available at quantity discounts with
bulk purchase for educational, business, or sales promotional use.
For information, please e-mail the Andrews McMeel Publishing
Special Sales Department: sales@amuniversal.com.

To all those I still carry with me

Contents

No matter how obsessed you've been with
your own vanishing, there will always be
someone who wants you whole.

—Hanif Abdurraqib

*

I understand I could hold onto the past or be happy.

—Dr. Maya C. Popa

HUM

memory: I have many appetites, but to be
where I once was hums the loudest

CURRENTS

what is a memory but two currents
pulling away from another
yes, I am here but I am also
every place I have held someone
that I love

GRASPING

when a name becomes past tense
only the wind can carry it
and we spend an entire lifetime
grasping onto that wind

SUMMER, A LITTLE YOUNGER

I pluck the wildflower
rising up from the soil
behind your ear—
this is a country
I want to live in

ODE TO *PUNISHER*, CONCLUDING IN A TWO-SECOND SERMON IN WHICH I BECOME THE RAIN
after "I Know the End" by Phoebe Bridgers

I am making sad music & of course what that means
is I have started praying again & not to any one thing
but to all my past selves & remembering who I was
becoming & just like one thing can change us—so
much of a song exists within one uttered phrase—like
the expelled breath filling up a single note to end a
hymn & at the 2:08 mark of "I Know the End" &
how when the sound becomes smoke I realize I have
seen the face of the end I'm heading toward & I have
known it since the beginning & I run to my god like
wind-soaked rain & I'm still running & the only thing
holier than perfection is carrying more grief than you
are capable of lifting & I am still being repaired & the
harvest was small this year & I've moved so far from
home I can't see the porchlight anymore & I have this
great habit of only letting people love the worst parts
of me & my chest is a flower in an earthquake & when
I open my mouth to relieve the tension in my chest a
small bird crumbles out & it stares into a vacant sky it
will never meet & I say *I know*

CARRY

there were many days
I did not believe I would
see another tomorrow—
here I am, on the eve
of another, unraveling
my loves & appreciations
knowing that while I carry
them, they also carry me

William Bortz

WALKING UNDER CITY LIGHTS, JUNE 2022

I press into my sadness
like a door, believing
there is light on the other side

HOW BADLY I WANT TO SEE

when I say forever
I'm saying tomorrow
I'm saying closer
I'm saying that pain is a whisper
watch as it unravels in the wind
time calls me to wilt
to live only off of memory
I want to be draped in the dust of the present
to see my skin pulled taut over my bones like a vibrant field
to see everything radiant
as though time has turned
its face away

MARKS

how euphoric a morning
to be breathing in warm air
laced with rain—to have dreamt
of hands so vibrantly I awoke
with their indents on my chest
to know love as something both
close and incredibly distant
I can only speak its name
while I am sleeping

HOW

how do we discern between the change we force
and the growth we desperately need

BOUQUET

at golden hour
the sky is shedding lavender
I open my throat to catch
such a brilliant departure

oh, to leave a bouquet
in your absence
what of love isn't this?

AWAY

birds build nests in my teeth
because I speak only of a home
that exists far away

TO MOVEMENT

watch how we move
like we are the storm
& not the thing running from it
see my clouds of breath
how they transform
I no longer want to build memories
longing is a sickness
I want to hold on to
things until I trust they exist
all I know of truth
is that it rarely changes
& when it does I become
undone

THE FIRST DEATH IS MEMORY

I am a sunrise—brief brilliance
color dripping like icemelt, like wet
bone. when I say I'm leaving I mean
I'm waiting; I mean when it's
quieter I'll try again; I mean I am
as uncertain about tomorrow as anyone
else is so I'm leaving you with something
to carry in your palms—like a bird, nursing
its feeble wing back into a sword
so to again cleave the sky into tangerine slices.
this is called beautiful damage; it's called the casualty of living—
is that not dying? no, the first death is memory
dropping out of all the ones kept by the people you love
I have no family here—the nest is on the tallest limb
I cannot fly or coast on rain-thick air.
it'll be tomorrow soon, and by then
you'll have forgotten I was ever here.

PERMANENT

what we don't know about the world
we look for in words
like touch—oh, touch
how a gentle thing
seems to go on
endlessly

SPRING POND, 2020

like dusk, like stardust,
like a strand of my lover's hair
draped in a moonbeam

gold, like worth,
like being held; not just for a short while

like being held forever

PRAYER, AFTERNOON

I sing to my wounds
and they open
what of healing
isn't turning hurt
into something
delicate

COUNTING AWAY

what I mean when I say I miss being young
is I don't remember what it's like to believe
in infinity. all I know are endings and I'm not
sure which to welcome and which to mourn.
innocence is something we are always
counting away from.

TATTERED

I understand that when the body
says sleep it means wait. it means
those soft things have a pulse of
their own. I add nothing to gentleness.
tomorrow is slowly fading, a
slivered moonbeam on a windowsill,
a tiny bird I cannot teach to fly.

APRIL, AND EVERYTHING IS STILL

God—
are you only a flicker
residual red haze lingering
as tail lights turn off the street leading home
the particles & dust keeping a
distant erupting star from becoming
the final morning
can the whites of your eyes
call suffering to be a wilting flame
if so, could you turn
and face me

FEEL

leaving: I am still holding on, from far away. can you feel me?

WRAP

change is the world
wrapping differently
around our tender bodies.
how are we to emerge
and remain soft?

GARDEN

what we don't know about the world
we look for in words

*

words like *dream*
in mine, I am still running

*

last time her hands were
on my body they didn't leave
until the sun came up;
they stayed until something
worth loving grew out of me

*

but also, to love is to bury
see: as I try to hide it
from the purest parts of me

*

the cigarette burns from dad
are starting to look like dandelions

*

this isn't the first time I've been a garden

*

time leaves its shadow over *everything*

*

every breath is a eulogy, as your face becomes mist

*

mom clips the bud just beneath the petal
and as it falls it transforms into a bird's wing

*

yes, I am still holding on to
the many things I have lost

*

the wing grows a bird
and goes to the water
to drink

*

mother hunched over her tomatoes
late afternoon sunbeams setting
her hair aflame
she ensures they don't touch the ground

*

this is where love begins

*

I am hoping to feel these things again

*

in this story,
I am the
bird

*

I started propagating plants again

*

how things are plucked
and expected to continue growing

*

this, too, is memory

*

continue growing
damn you.
continue growing

PRAYER, 3AM

when we think of trauma
we think of doors bolted
thunder undressing the silence
an unraveling
is there an end or an undoing
is there light
there must be light

REACHING THROUGH

I am constantly dreaming
of elsewhere

like a waterfall emptying
itself forever

perhaps it is true joy is a circle
waiting to be filled in

the palette being what we
aren't able to see of the world

TIMBRE

birds scream across the sky like an emergency
in another life I was a transmission pole—
I was energy, the blade slicing a flooding sky
into wet slices—I was something

here I am aging
like tomorrow is a dream. here I am
trying to see appreciation as both
the phantom pain and the initial severing
removed from any damage I am wind—
not always cautious, but *always*

press an ear to an apple tree
you cannot hear the fruit growing—
all you hear is the tree dying
to be a god is to name small violences
as necessary fingers on an unabridged body—
to be a god is to define suffering as *human*

William Bortz

PRAYER, SUNRISE

today is ripe with many loves
I will cling to them tightly

MINERAL WATER

how great it is to miss things
it means *we were there, we
felt something*

to be simply
surviving and feel anything
at all is a miracle

walking
beneath cherry blossoms
in the humid June air

walking at midnight to get
a slice of pizza from Big Tomato—
your eyes blending in with the
neon signs

mother, quiet and
patient, her face drunk with light

all these many small hungerings
I cannot seem to set down

there is no moon like the one
I weep beneath, other than
the moon we weep beneath

William Bortz

WHERE DUST NEVER COLLECTS

when I say love, I mean
I wait at the door for
you to arrive; I mean
the walls of my chest
are decorated with your
pictures; I mean it's
safe here

BUILDING A COUNTRY

love is as small as whisper
see how our hands touch
like we're building a country
I've fallen in love with your shadow again
when you're away, I dance with it

IN REMEMBERING

lightning flashes
just beyond a
ripe and swaying field
thick as honey
because of its distance
it is an empty mouth

I consider what has once been whispered
a name, a date, an expiration

I recall my mother's wheat-gold hair
bending—just before twilight
in a midsummer breeze
few things are as sweet
as moments of rebirth
air so heavy with moisture
I collect it in my palms and drink

another flicker against
the darkening underbelly of clouds
followed closely by the shadow
of a tremble, then

quiet

MAGIC

to hold the people you love
is magic. it is in this way
we fit an eternity into the
pinprick of our lives.

PALMS

grief: this impossible thing! this whole time I
thought I was holding you in my palms, but it
is you who hold me.

MOTHER IN THE VALLEY, 1974

when dusk lingers to the point
of violence I consider you

decades ago, in the mouth of
some red rock valley

unaware of how the world
would turn its face away from you

you pictured, staring into
its cooling eyes

believing in so much
I can hardly recognize you

LAMENT, 2AM

how do we grieve something we never had
but longed for to the point of suffering

GOOD IN A GLASS, GOOD ON GREEN

sometimes, at golden hour, I imagine
I am where you are

our breathing echoing
a flower in the thicket

everything sounds as real as it is

the sun burning itself out
behind the countryside

your hand on the nape of my neck
your smile a birdsong

PRAYER, DUSK

I am holding on to memory
like it is my breathing
so many lives I have lived
that I didn't believe
I deserved

PLEASE CARRY ME

love is spoken of as though it doesn't speak
for itself, like it doesn't have its own wet mouth.
the palm of my hand swallows yours and a prairie
shudders, the wispy ends of your hair dances
behind your ear and a cloud empties of rain;
i whisper your name into a stale afternoon &
you vanish. this tongue knows only erosion, knows
taking. you appear to me in a dream as if your
chest is rising and falling beside me; this loneliness
is a jewel i have pulled from a shadow. i am so small
& you are mostly brave. will you please carry me?

AN ODE TO RIBS
after "Ribs" by Lorde

I, too, have felt the embrace of
a small love that I believed
could never outgrow itself
it's not enough to remember
I want the pulp on my tongue
—the laughter, the wonder
my body a full moon in an empty night sky
radiant and permanent

BECOMING

the color of becoming
the hue of laughter
drape me in sunbeams
call me by my good name
say what I am is growing
watch the flowers bloom as I walk by

I'M SAYING I STILL DREAM ABOUT CALLING OUT TO YOU

if I ask for yesterday to come back
I'm saying those gentle words
are still humming in my throat

PRAYER, AFTER YOU LEFT SUDDENLY

if there is life after this one
let it be long and merciful

OIL LAMP

mother: a ghost in a screen
a whisper through a window
your hands are holding a saint's last breath
I feel the lament through your fingertips
I fear my memory is fading like a spent oil lamp—
are you the landscape shrouded in fog?
light hidden in the belly of weather
when I see your face in movement
will it be an epiphany or a picture
color returning to countryside;
the smeared flowers gaining back a hue of laughter
is brilliance something as small as the wind of breath
being so close it becomes the only thing

MIRROR

the body is a delicate machine
a bird plummeting from a sky
that once held it; a rapture
everything I believe about the body
is its shadow I am chasing—
it wraps around my fingers like smoke
I cannot catch it

DRIFT

my purpose is not
to drift
but to push hard
against the waves
crashing over me

ANXIOUS, EARLY 2021

when we think about stillness
how the flower opens only while no one is watching
that movement is but a *waiting*
a star decorating the palette of twilight

what happens while we skim the sky for another bulb
of light

not stillness—panic
a violence like opening a door
only to find a wall
and not an exit

there could never be stillness
we simply continue quietly opening doors
making sure no one can see our hands trembling
searching for our way out

RESERVOIR

to remember: to reach your hands back
into old water, to wish it clearer, to savor
its taste on your tongue, to steal
a small reservoir, to see your
reflection in the still surface,
to count the smallest ripples
of change

TINY RIVERS EVERYWHERE

to think of how often gentleness has saved a life
the slow unfurling of spring, the sweet-thick air

daisies, tiny rivers everywhere, more light
how this thing that cannot be held

can carry so many back to the choice
of staying alive

COMMUNAL

grief is the phantom limb
that I reach to feel
but catch air
the incessant circulating
of blood and air that
mix more violently
in some more than
others, yet we all
feel it in our parts
that others have lost

POEM ON WRITING ABOUT MY FATHER

I stand in front of the poem
and I am quieter

I am sure the world would've looked larger
from atop your shoulders

each night I fall asleep asking a question
and wake up before I find the answer

all I wanted to know is where your ashes are going to be spread
without having to ask someone

when the poem comes out
it is only a shard of light

the blood on my hand
is still warm

SOFT HANDS

when I say forever, I am saying
tomorrow; I'm saying closer

I am saying that pain is whisper
that the wind unravels

BAD WING

I am healing, which also means
that I'm singing songs I used to
love again, that I'm building
bridges back to places I haven't
visited in awhile, that I'm holding
my shadow like a bird with a bad wing,
that slowly I am believing I was
never a burden

STILL EVEN TODAY

am I not always
carrying a tiny
eternity with me?
the memory in which
you spoke my name
on a fragile morning
never ends—I am
still hearing it.

AND I OPEN

if anxiety is the fear of outcomes
I am carrying so many potential endings
call me a graveyard, a late-summer tree
sprinting to its wilting
I often do not believe newness could be on the
other side of this door. but what else could be
waiting there

William Bortz

THE ENEMY RESTS IN THE SHADE

but when I leave / what will I be remembered for /
I counted my blessings like rainfall / I stood, mouth
open, pointed toward the heavens / the truth is not
everything clings to lips like honey from our home
country / time builds holes in memory like an eager
gun / yes, builds / like an immunity; like the hope to
unremember; like the tension of understanding that to
heal is to find what first caused the pain and lean into
it like the shade of a willow tree on a Midwest July
evening / say: weep; say: bone; say: utility; say: when
the body says sleep it means wait / these rules and their
consequences / a slow parade on an endless stretch of
road / our becoming is no tree in the distance / but a
mirage of clearwater / the end to thirst is always more
fulfilling in thought than in practice / we find kinship
in toil / and are a child to our nostalgia / come, affixed
to your intimacy / everything is soft when seen at a
distance / and everything is out of reach / even you,
your slow breathing, and its prairies rising and falling
with a noon-wind / if there ever was an end / it's there
/ in the clearsunned palm of a quiet war / know that
when I was asked to be brave / I recalled myself the
enemy / and lost

OPTIMISM

I would like to think
that there will be
a day when I think less
about endings, and more
about beginnings

RISK

can we trust memory
how its branches
reach out in so many
directions. how do we
know which are sturdy
enough to hold our
weight

UNMARKED

I consider what it means to make the bed
for someone you love

there is a whole country here
I believe in little else

what is longing if it isn't for something impossible
the world to be unmoving for just a moment

sleep here and miss nothing
I'll slow my breathing for you

pull the sheets tight
it's safe to dream here

nothing has been touched

CLASP

father—a crow on a humming light pole,
despondent and dissociated; knows my face,
my misdeeds, but not much else
I named him *thornbush, matchbox, monsoon*
for the way he ignites—suddenly. there is
only you—a room with impossible exits,
windows of lightning—a memory I clasp
like a single hollowed note until he flaps
his good wings and becomes smoke.

PRAYER, BEFORE

God,
why do you make
everything so fragile
I often doubt you made hands
that can hold without
breaking. I hope I am wrong.
if so, will you guide me
into them

William Bortz

MANY

all I know of war
is what never made
it home

GHOST(S)

I am healing—what I mean is
I am digging up old violences and calling them to be soft
what I mean is I watched the sun faint
beneath low-lying hills and looked for morning
what I mean is I looked in the mirror and didn't tremble
what I mean is I'm not a ghost anymore

INDENTS

I am holding on to everything sweet
the fingerprints the sun leaves on my skin
how you speak my name slowly like a warm rain
each flower that blooms from my breathing
the way in which something so vibrant can be so fragile

LOVE SONG

shouldn't love have some qualifications
shouldn't it bend the magnetic force of the earth like a song
shouldn't it be a slow drip of lightning in a silent field

NIGHT POEM

what of our many constellations
what of our distant light—
we are only a cosmos
in a dark sea
pressing back against
the night

BREAKAGE

love: when you say *love* do you mean *breakage*; one day inevitably, one of us will be left holding it on our own. a vase of flowers sitting still on the table

SPACE

our tiny eternity set between
two quiet stars is all I ever
wanted to find in a sky
seemingly too large for me

PRAYER, MORNING

I am thinking about what I've been given
this body and its rivers
an infinite number of beginnings
a light that never goes out

AND TIME MARCHES FORWARD

the whole day vanishes with one deep breath.
today, the yellow pendants on the oak tree
never knew the sun. with one deep breath
I rework the whole day. I didn't wear my
pain like a pendant. I never vanished. when
the sun crested the low hill I named it yellow.
I breathed deep and was handed everything.
the blanket of night reworked my bones

BELIEF

the heart is strong
it can mend what breaks
in your hands

William Bortz

DELIGHT, 2020

my troubles sprinkle over me—a soft rain
I do not consider
how quickly they could grow

is this ignorance, or delight

maybe nothing is as big
or as heavy as I am told
it was going to be

what feels like a sea
is just a mouthful
I'm lying to myself again

your name, that song
I am looking for air in it
but it, too, is gasping

what I need is formless
how do I take it with me

GOOD MEMORY

I'm at my best when buried
in the mouth of a good memory. when my
laughter blooms into a bouquet—when it's
held in hands that have held me when I
needed it most

William Bortz

REAPPEAR

when we talk about missing someone
we are talking about their ghost
we're pulling color from whatever
is most vibrant to fill in what
isn't there

THIS, TOO, IS A DOOR

every ending is a door
I press my palms into
& decide to either turn
& paint myself still
into a memory
or continue forward

William Bortz

EVERY DAY I GROW SMALLER

I am just this body
waiting to be more
the horizon; an endpoint, a departure
a quiet place
I say my name and only hear the echo
watch as I dismantle myself
and become a memory
listen as I slowly
count until I reach
infinity

PASSING

see how dusk fades to night
like it's an arrival, not a departure
see how the stars are wrapped
in lavender as they hum
such a soft goodbye
as though it was meant to be
in this way, not all things
are meant to remain

CHURCH

The body is written about because it is
one of the few things that can be understood.
It rains and the drops finding windowsills recites *newness*;
spring rests its head on the cold chest of winter & I wonder
why I am unchanged. If you peel open my sternum on
a heavy sunday morning, you may see
god for the first time. I am a temple, a church
in the way the light there only exists if I
carry it out on my teeth.

KALEIDOSCOPE

I am a kaleidoscope of moments
all my loves and fears living in
this same body. What I hold on to
is what kept me going
are the ones that feel infinite
the ones in which I was loved

WANT

sometimes I forget how badly I longed
for all that I have
sometimes I forget that this body is a machine—
faulty and untrustworthy
I give all I have for something
and forget its name before the season ends
the wanting part of me always shows its teeth

ALL WE KNOW OF DEATH IS ITS MUSIC

trying to speak your name is
like throwing a fist in a dream—all air and no impact

we are made in his image
exuberant and split

though your body is gone
I can still feel your hands

wind strikes the hanging chime
the porch door opens and slams shut

there is no one there
but it sounds like you

I will hold on to this—
some only get silence

PAINTING

what is there left to say
we go on breathing &
paint the breath of those
we lose into every dusk
hoping it'll open a door
we can walk through

SLOWLY

we eventually become all of the things we miss
I am a melting July evening wrapped in ribbons of twilight
young starlight cupping my cheekbones—
my sun-kissed skin still warm
whatever worries I have, they're long gone
so far away they could only be a bad dream

William Bortz

ODE TO THE SMOKE I AM BECOMING

to live means to slowly evaporate
I've held so many things
that have become left behind
watch as I unravel heaven
from a vibrant sunset
& hold the clouds
in my teeth like the
names of people I haven't
spoken the name of in
years—I fear God
every time I breathe
I press into his chest
what I'm saying is
prayer is a language
speaking only appreciation
if I ask for yesterday
to come back, I'm saying
all those gentle words
are still humming in my throat;
I'm saying undo whatever
sadness I am carrying
before I become smoke

THE SADDEST THING I KNOW

is that we will lose everything we give a name to
& will recite those names from dawn to dusk
calling them to come back
until one day we sing a new song

AN ODE TO THE FIRST TIME I DANCED AND FELT SOMETHING

put me back in a car heated to a severe discomfort by
the fading July sun—the steering wheel hot iron on my
palms. a song spilling out of the blown speakers, some
pop track that makes people who don't dance want to
dance. how these simple things give life to parts of us
that have never taken a breath & we sing so off-key it
sounds only like screaming & the neon signs and lit
billboards light up the packed interior like a nightclub.
warm bodies shouting hallelujah whenever a cool
breeze pours in one window & out another. it is in these
moments when our sorrow and shortcomings are like
a tree in the distance. and with each hallelujah sang in
a language everybody speaks, we hope that tree is also
praying to whatever small blessing it is holding & that
it is enough to make it dance beneath fading light

MAYBE

When the body says sleep it means wait;
it means try again tomorrow; it means
trust things may be softer. I dream of running,
of rivers. I dream of not being scared to
move. Maybe tomorrow I will.

YESTERDAY'S ACHE

Growth means I turn yesterday's ache
into laughter. It means pain won't
become something soft if you
don't hold it a little while. It means
my love is a prairie & I spend
afternoons lying in its tall grass.
It means I am strong even when
I don't feel strong. It means if
I can't go on, I'll ask someone
to carry me.

PAST TENSE

it is not that I want to fix you
I want to fix the things around you
the world, banging on our door
the mirror, how it houses only violence
all the many names that have grown past-tense
how badly I wish to recite them
and see a face in return
and the hands that take
oh, and how they take

William Bortz

REACTIONS

my hands pressed to a thin veil of light unfold a memory.
Mother, when you send your body off, could the rest of you live here?
my tongue lingers over the memory and blossoms hemlock.
we speak the same language; we recite the same songs; our bones
are equally as sharp. I wrinkle myself into something small—
a marble, a tooth, a pinprick of light, I must become a beginning or
anything without a sour memory.
you've wished yourself away so many times you've become a mist;
your name, a stray cloud in an open sky; recalling your touch,
a cloverleaf beneath timber. for those left behind to rediscover
moments—
unthreading the multitude of hues from dusk to find what built it—
only in small ways: puffs of quiet flame, an atom
undressing & pressing its hands to its body; one single note, held
but shaken; the whimper of a moonbeam adorning an empty
field. we know the exit, its inscription reads on everything; but
its entrance, that is where you will be, that is where we are going.

THANKFULNESS

all I know of pain
is what I've turned it into
long nights drunk on moonlight
laughter, warm bodies
with gentle words

William Bortz

TEMPORARY

each star is a memory
a face, a touch, a quiet word
on long nights
I wrap myself in them
pulled up to my chin
& dream of faraway places
being close

NOT ABOUT A GUN, II

I am a citizen of the country called panic.
it is here I rinse my empathy; my neighbor
jumps & I follow. the cherry blossoms have
already come & gone to bed; I question what
work is left for me to do. another hero
becomes mist. a scream is heard a block over
& every light flickers on. I am facing outward
& trying to pronounce all I am a witness to.
all that escapes my teeth is an unintelligible
shout & the city ignites.

VIBRANCY

wish: I speak and a flower blooms somewhere lacking vibrancy

SUMMER, 2016

stay because the flowers
are going to bloom soon
stay because they're most
vibrant when sown into your hair
stay because the first time
you said my name dusk opened
like a door & you said this
never has to end &
I believed you

SUMMER CLOUDS

the sky is so still—a mountain buried in the rain
I just want it to open

this sounds like a riddle but it's a wish
I want your bubblegum-pink-tipped fingers
wrapped around my sunburnt skin

time is so large it's immovable

when I say I want it all back
I mean I tell myself things that aren't true
just to get by
what I mean is I want it all
I'll call parts of me to evaporate for it back

I want the sky to open but to remain still
and to fit a tall, sprouting summer cloud on my tongue

I am simply asking to feel something and for the
world to wait for a moment so I can carry it

EXIT

how do I survive myself
I've been praying to
my memories for an exit
I may have missed—
that one time you spoke
my name and I could fly
I want to live there

CONSIDERING THE WAYS IN WHICH I COULD FAIL, WEDDING DAY

I could be taller, I think
and I don't have as many teeth as I once did
these are the things I considered on the day of my wedding
to be bonded to loss—I am evaporating
the bouquet was too heavy, my wife
had to pass it off; of what burdens
become light when discarded
I am told the sunflowers were local
what a frantic continent
whenever I sweat I begin to question everything
can you carry this name
there are no roots
it is all top-heavy and leaning
all stem and no blossom
I don't think this eternity has any sun
how will the fruit grow
how will the flowers survive
without any good light

SELF-PORTRAIT OF THE SENSES IN DEPARTURE

there is a mountain I am at the foothills of—
it looks big, looks *impossible*, looks
empty like father's hands, blocks out
the sun. father, I remember the sound
of your mustache scraping my forehead as
you kissed the bridge of my nose—sounded
like raindrops hitting tin, sounded like a car crash
sounded like the hollow sound through
a payphone receiver. somehow your
absence is larger than you were &
I say this now, standing still in your shadow.

LAMENT, AUTUMN 2019

afternoon spills in my lap
a pile of dethreaded dandelion leaves
you were once whole
as I held you in my mouth
but upon growing cold
in your presence
I shredded you
between my teeth
such is my heart, oh, God

ON THE COAST, AT THE EDGE OF THE WORLD, AT THE CUSP OF WONDER

give me the language
words finding the tip of my tongue
like a mountain burrowing through high clouds
home has always been here—
just hidden behind; undrinkable water
in my head and in my thoughts,
father stands behind mother, peering over her shoulder
she seeds sweet peppers—he wonders how
something could ever be so soft
and he doesn't desire to break it
I sprint toward my God like a monsoon
my hair, dripping, falls to my shoulders
to be in the presence of anything holy is to be sinking
the memories rapture my understanding of time
a new bruise today for a decade-old bashing
all of this remembering like a choir of voices
losing their breath

REMEDY

I know so little
I am holding on to the space between

sorrow is thick tonight
I see stringed lights strung on a balcony

and hear music playing
over soft voices

this dilutes the sadness
I do not have an answer as to why

but that rarely matters

FUTURE,

I am walking through the dark
not holding on to it
there is light on the horizon
to which I call the future
and I see myself there

NO ONE DIED THAT DAY

today I am daydreaming about apple orchards
and the first instance I loved you to the point of invention
when it is too quiet I think about tiny things
the stem keeping the fruit from fainting
pockets of light where dust morphs into gold
a stray strand of your hair caught in the neck of my shirt
when god speaks people die and others are born
that vanishing line separating the two is the tiniest thing—
when your fingers grabbed the apple and pulled it to your mouth
god fell silent and no one died that day

SOFT, FREE

if I were to leave this earth tomorrow
I would remember your touch how the sky remembers
the flap of a bird's wing

William Bortz

THE REVOLUTION HAS TAKEN ON A HUE OF

laughter; flower petals sauntering down
from their high clouds; sun-painted wicker
baskets—a cornucopia of overflowing
hands; dusk walks beneath undressing
elms; the smoke of breath, a stream of
vibrant fruit juice filling the reservoir
of an uncalloused palm; light-drenched faces;
dust-filled beams of light loved into becoming soft,
adored into becoming golden; truth like a window,
your full reflection, mother's wisdom, father's
hands as true as a tree trunk; no bells, only
a choir of voices like sunrise over low hills; a
spinning cosmos like a kaleidoscope of old dreams,
in them no one is running, in them the
sky peppered with stars doesn't open
like a hungry mouth, in them the only shadow
is peeling from the unbreathing body of
what has been hurting us

MAPLE LEAF

these small beloved things—
a good leaf, an absurdly
large fruit, a spent candle,
the pinky finger of your love
yes, we sit beneath a wild cosmos
and ask to see it up close
but watching you hold up
a maple leaf in front of your face
joyous beyond measure
that it's the same size
as your head
makes me never want to look away

ON A WALK, MID-SPRING

Once again the world is
being wrapped in a blanket
of warmth. Beneath it,
fox lilies, lemongrass,
& geraniums are erupting.
Their small hands lifted
in prayer, their posture
is thankfulness.
I kneel beside them
letting the sun plant
roses in the high of
my cheekbones.

WAITING

safe means the fractured bits
& lovely things that I call
this body can touch—
a mosaic, a discovery
it means I don't need
to watch out the window
I know you're coming back

TO BE KNOWN

to forgive is to remember
that even us, at our best
can sometimes cause hurt
can sometimes press too firmly
& in those moments what
we longed for most was to
be known, was to be
forgiven

AGAIN

there must be a way
to remember pain without
feeling it again

I need to understand who I am becoming

how do I paint myself back
into the oil painting of a war I lost
without having to pick up the gun

William Bortz

THREE TO THE RIGHT, FOUR TO THE LEFT

is the key to coping somewhere in memory
I am holding on to the good mornings

your hands
soft—first/before
they began tightening
you, recalling things
air in your voice, sweet air
dancing from coffee machine
to table, your eyes soft as plums

do you remember you are here
have the wires crossed again

today your footsteps go unheard
the fridge hums, the dishwasher rumbles
the paper in your hands bent crudely
and unopened

the thought, I'm sure, hasn't crossed your mind
you, smiling—a different person
is the key believing
you're still here

TRANSFORM

I watch the sun blow out
its seeds like a ripe dandelion
dusk has become so cold
I can't hold it in my palms
something somewhere has to be beginning
change makes me distant
change makes everything untouchable

PRESENT

oh, to recall every sweet thing
that has dripped from your lips
& not forget how it tasted
the first time it turned your tongue
into a sanctuary

PINING

I am still learning to
nurture all that is in
my hands before pining
after what is not

A CRACK IN THE CONCRETE, A GORGE

hours after dusk & the violent sky is softened by the
shadow of clouds & there are constant thuds as moths
and other insects throw themselves into the stringed
lights draped over the balcony railing & I couldn't be
convinced I am in the middle of my life & what I am
saying is that I am scared & what I am saying is I most
often can't see what is in front of me & the glory of
what love can sometimes mean & the possibility of
what love can become & I watch the switch lights in
the distance touch the clouds so gently they stand still
for a moment & my wife sits on the couch just inside
sipping her tea & the only thing between us is memory

SUMMER, AFTER

this world without you feels small
I miss you standing in a June sun
pointing upward toward the heavens
at a cloud you say looks much
like the entrance to eternity
stray sunbeams igniting
some field someplace I
cannot find without you
leading me there

INTIMACY

when I say love I mean
I want to start a fire
with your bones. I mean
if the body is a machine
I want to dismantle it
& drink its oil. I mean
when you're not near
I recite your name like
a prayer to the moon
& wrap myself in the echo.

LAMENT, LATE EVENING

love, of all things,
is a shadow
how do you keep
exuberant things
close to you
without them
becoming a shadow
even now,
I am growing dim

William Bortz

IMPENETRABLE DELIGHTS

these small joys—
these impenetrable delights
upon knitting them together
they become a monument
which is named the body

RUSS

while we are here
let us laugh to the point
of blooming

let us leave something behind
to be plucked

ACKNOWLEDGMENTS

Deep gratitude to the editors of the publications where some of these poems first appeared, sometimes in different forms.

To Estee Zandee: Thank you. To Trinity McFadden and the rest of the crew at The Bindery: Huge thank you for believing in me and my work. It's a gift to be able to work with you.

To my community: Thank you for keeping me present.

To Chelsie, my wife: Thank you for your joy and your love.

Reader, thank you.

NOTES AND CREDITS

The epigraph from Hanif Abdurraqib is from *They Can't Kill Us Until They Kill Us*. The epigraph from Dr. Maya C. Popa is from the poem "The Present Speaks of Past Pain" in her book *Wound Is the Origin of Wonder*, first published in the *Adriot Journal*.

"Ode to *Punisher*, Concluding in a Two-Second Sermon in Which I Become the Rain" was written after Phoebe Bridgers's song "I Know the End" off her album *Punisher*, specifically beginning at the 2:08 minute mark.

"The First Death Is Memory" was first published in *Brave Voices* magazine.

"Timbre" was first published in *Parentheses Journal*.

"In Remembering" was first published by Central Avenue in *[Dis]Connected* Volume 2.

"Good in a Glass, Good on Green" borrows its title from a lyric in the song "Slow Burn" by Kacey Musgraves off the album *Golden Hour*.

"An Ode to Ribs" is written after the song "Ribs" by Lorde off the album *Pure Heroine*.

"The Enemy Rests in the Shade" was first published in *The Lumiere Review*.

"All We Know of Death" was first published in *Random Sample Review*.

"Not About a Gun, ll" is a continuation of the poem "Not About a Gun" published in the book *The Grief We're Given* by me.

"Three to the Right, Four to the Left" borrows its title from a piece of dialogue spoken in season 2, episode 4 of *Stranger Things*.

ABOUT THE AUTHOR

William Bortz is the author of a previous poetry collection, *The Grief We're Given* (Central Avenue). His poems have appeared in *Brave Voices* magazine, *The Lumiere Review*, *Empty Mirror*, *Okay Donkey*, and others. He is a poetry reader for *Longleaf Review* and a part of the volunteer curating team for Button Poetry. He lives in the Midwest with his wife.